THE LAST WORD

IN
MEMORIAM

THE LAST WORD

Tombstone Wit and Wisdom

Nicola Gillies

DOVETAIL
BOOKS

TO LIVE IN THE HEARTS OF THOSE
WE LEAVE BEHIND IS NOT TO DIE.

Copyright © 1997, DoveTail Books
Design copyright © Ziga Design

Produced in association with Saraband Inc.

ISBN 1-889461-02-4

Printed in China

2 4 6 8 9 7 5 3 1

 CONTENTS

🍂 FOREWORD

One of our earliest forms of literary expression, the epitaph offers the reader a glimpse of the past and, perhaps, a universal truth. Although tombstone inscriptions may be private tributes from the bereaved, they are also public declarations, often written with the reader in mind and addressing him or her directly.

While some epitaphs are concise records of factual information, others offer more descriptive details of the lives of the deceased. Presenting the reader with an impression of character or circumstances, epitaphs celebrate the lives and achievements and commemorate the passing of those who have gone before us. These everlasting memories are poignant, hopeful, even humorous farewells to those who left this world in a variety of ways. Whether their deaths were accidental, induced, expected or tragic, the inscriptions were all written with a common purpose—to record the ending of a life.

This intriguing collection of last words includes final tributes to the famous and infamous, rich and poor, young and old, forgotten and anonymous, and even their much-loved pets, spanning many centuries and countries.

Journey through time with these immortal tributes and meet the men, women and children who have departed this world for their final resting places.

I

DEARLY DEPARTED, SADLY MISSED

Poignant tributes to much-loved relatives and friends

🖋 THE POETRY OF LOVE

My dearest dust, could not thy hasty day
Afford thy drowsy patience leave to stay
One hour longer: so that we may either
Sit up, or go to bed together?
But since thy finished labor hath possest
Thy weary limbs with early rest,
Enjoy it sweetly: and thy widow bride
Shall soon repose here by thy slumbering side.
Whose business, now, is only to prepare
My nightly dress, and call to prayer:
Mine eyes wax heavy and the day grows cold.
Draw, draw the closed curtains, and make room:
My dear, my dearest dust; I come, I come.
　　　—Sir William Dyer, d. 1641
　　　Colmworth, Bedfordshire

My Ann, my all, my Angel Wife
My dearest one, my love, my life
I cannot sigh or say farewell
But where thou dwellest I will dwell.
　　　—d. 1849
　　　Williamsburg, Virginia

8

Where flies my wife oh lovely once and fair
Her face cast in the mould of beauty, where
Her eyes all radiance her cheeks like snow
Whose cheeks once tinctured with a purple glow
Where those ivory teeth and lips of celestial sound
Her lips like lilys set with roses round

Where's that soft marble breast white neck and where
That all of woman past description fair—
All sunk alas in everlasting night
Earth take her bones chaste soul she smiles at rest
Whilst her image lives on immortal in my breast.
    —*d. 1779*

Could grateful love recall the fleeting breath,
Or fond affection soothe relentless death,
Then had this stone ne'er claimed a social tear
Nor read to thoughtless man a lesson here
As those we love decay, we die in part
String after string, is sever'd from the heart.
    —*d. 1839*

My glass is run
With graceful and engaging mien
She trod the carpet and the green
With such refulgent virtues deckt
As gained her wide and warm respect.
Prim health sat blooming on her cheeks
Till Fortune play'd her cruel freaks

Her limbs in tort'ring pains confin'd
That wreck'd her joints tho not her Mind
By faith and patience fortified
The rudest tempest to abide
'Bove which she soar'd to realms of bliss
When Jesus hail'd her with a kiss.
    —*d. 1791*

There's not an hour
Of day or dreaming night but I am with thee;
There's not a breeze but whispers of thy name,
And not a flower that sleeps beneath the moon
But in its fragrance tells a tale of thee.
    —*Jane Placide, American actress, d. 1835*

SORROWING SPOUSES

A Husband kind a Father dear
A Friend in need lies buried here.
   —d. 1855

Farewell dear wife my life is past
My love to you while life did last,
And after me no sorrows take
But love my orphans for my sake.
   —d. 1867

Here lies the remains of H. P. Nichol's wife
Who mourned away her natural life.
She mourned herself to death for her man
While he was in the service of Uncle Sam.
   —d. 1863

The Greatest Person
I Have Ever Known.
   —Elizabeth Cothran, d. 1925
     from her husband Francis E. Harrison.

A loving wife
And tender mother
Left this base world
To enjoy the other.
    —*Anon.*

She was more to me
Than I expected.
    —*d. 1882*

Lo! Where this silent marble weeps,
A friend, and wife, a mother sleeps.
    —*d. 1806*

Dearest Thomas thou art gone,
Thy kind heart I miss.
You did not say Good-bye, Tom,
Or give me the parting kiss.
    —*Anon.*

LITTLE ONES LOST

This lovely flower of fairest bloom
Thus early met a sudden doom
From his fond parents torn away
Now lives and blooms in endless day.
 —*d. 1845*
  Putney, Vermont

The less of this cold world, the more of Heaven:
The briefer life, the earlier Immortality.
 —*Toronto, Canada*

It is so soon that I am done for,
I wonder what I was begun for.
 —*17th Century, Cheltenham*

His last words were unspoken
He never said 'Good-bye'
He was gone before he knew it
And only God knows why.
 —*Anon.*

Our Little Jacob
Has been taken away from the Earthy Garden
To Bloom
In a superior Flower-pot
Above.
   —*Anon.*

This lovely bud, so young and fair,
Call'd hence by early doom,
Just came to show how sweet a flower
In Paradise might bloom.
   —*Richmond, Virginia
      from* Annals of the Poor

This innocence whose corpse lies here
It was Belov'd of Parents Dear.
   —*d. 1759*

Short was my time, the longer is my rest
God took me hence because He thought it best.
   —*Anon.*

 SOULMATES

Rest in peace
until we meet again.
—*Anon.*

We part to meet again,
What a joyful thought.
—*Chicago, Illinois*

Down the lanes of memory
The lights are never dim
Until the stars forget to shine
We shall remember her.
—*Anon.*

We often sit and think of you,
We often speak your name;
There is nothing left to answer,
But your photo in the frame.
—*Anon.*

And how it made by bosom heave
   To hear my dearest sister breathe
   And God to carry out his plans,
   Caused her to die within my hands.
And now dear Saviour please adore
   Her mother, aged eighty-four;
   Look down from on high
   And bless her ere she die.
     —*Anon.*

And in her memory we think we find
These accents uttered at this time.
Companions, you who once were mine,
Unto you I speak by the hand of time.
Yes! unto you who once were joined
Unto me by Friendship's coin,
Yea, unto you I now do speak,
Although my eyes are closed in sleep.
Here lies the remnants of your friend
Beneath this grassy mound;
And flowers may deck and flowers may bloom,
And flowers may wither on this mound,
Here stands my Tomb.
     —*Washington, Connecticut*

 FAITHFUL FRIENDS

Here lie the bones of a poor dog
Renowned for faith and bravery;
He died by hostile hands incog.
His name was Pompey Savery.
   —*Massachusetts.*

Rastas
The smartest
most lovable
Monkey
that ever lived.
   —*Hartsdale, New York*

ROSA

My first Jersey Cow
Record 2 lbs. 15 ozs. Butter
From 18 qts. 1 day milk.
   —*Evergreen Cemetery, Central Village, Connecticut.*

HEROES OF BATTLE

*D*ulce et decorum est pro patria mori.
[It is sweet and honorable to die for one's country.]
     —*Horace, Odes, III. ii.13.*

*T*o the world he was a soldier
To me he was the world.
     —*Anon.*

*I*n loving memory of our dear brother Richard,
who went to the War in the cause of Peace
and died fighting, without hate,
that love might live.
     —*Died in World War I*

*S*leep on, dear Howard, in your foreign grave,
Your life to your country you nobly gave,
Though we did not see you to say goodbye,
Now in God's keeping you safely lie.
     —*Private Howard Pruden, Mapleton, Canada*
      Died in World War I

We mourn and lament our brave youth
In one deep and national wail,
Who rushed to support our dear old flag
In its hour of deepest travail.
 —*William P. Eames, d. 1863 in the American Civil War*

When things were at their worst
he would go up and down in the trenches cheering the men,
when danger was greatest
his smile was loveliest.
 —*Edward Wyndham Tennant, 4th Battalion,*
  Grenadier Guards
  Died in World War I

Beneath this stone rests the body
of a British warrior
Unknown by name or rank.
 —*Tomb of the Unknown Soldier, d. 1920*
  Westminster Abbey, London

A soldier of the great war known unto God.
 —*Epitaph for unknown soldiers in World War I*

🪽 THE FINAL VOYAGE

Rocks and storms I'll fear no more,
When on that eternal shore.
Drop the anchor! Furl the sail!
I am safe within the Vail.
    —*Anon.*

I lost my life in the raging Seas
A Sovereign God does as he please.
The Kittery friends they did appear
And my remains lie buried here.
    —*Margaret Hills, d. 1803*

Long did my native powers
The dangerous ocean brave;
Protected by my God
At home I make my grave.
    —*d. 1804*

The Boreas' blasts and Boistrous waves
Have tost me to and fro
In spite of both, by God's decree
I harbor here below.
While I do now at Anchor ride
With many of our Fleet
Yet once again I must set Sail
My Admiral Christ to meet.
        —d. 1767
            Madison, Connecticut.

Twelve times the great Atlantic cross'd,
    To Fortune paying court:
In many a terrible Tempest toss'd,
    But now I'm safe in Port.
Yet is my Course not ended here,
    Through faith in Christ I trust.
My sins forgiv'n I shall appear
    Among the Good and Just.
        —d. 1784

WORDS OF COMFORT

To live in the hearts of those we leave behind
is not to die.
  —*Lytham St. Annes, Lancashire*

To die, is but to live forever.
  —*d. 1835*

Adieu my friends weep not for me
Long have I stemmed life's troubled sea
But now redeem'd from sin and woe
I rest where peaceful waters flow.
  —*d. 1844*

Death is not an eternal sleep,
Therefore my friends you need not weep;
But look by faith beyond the grave,
That you some peace of soul may have.
  —*d. 1803*

Surviving friends, although you mourn,
Let this console, I shall return:
The righteous judge can by his word
Bring me triumphing with the LORD.
        —*Anon.*

If there is a world above, he is in bliss;
If there is not he made the most of this.
        —*Anon.*

Weep not my friends as you pass by,
Beneath this stone my body lies,
My soul is gone in yonder skies,
To live with those that's prepared to die.
        —*Anon.*

Why do we mourn departing friends
Or shake at death's alarms?
Tis but the voice that Jesus sends
To call them to his arms.
        —*d. 1814*

ASHES TO ASHES

How loved, how valued once avails thee not
To whom related or by whom begot;
A heap of dust alone remains of thee
Tis all thou are, and what we all must be.
    —d. 1796

O Death all eloquent, you only prove
What dust we dote on when we creatures love.
    —from "Eloise to Abelard," *Alexander Pope*

Although she is dead she invites you to come
Look you in the churchyard and read it with care
Remember it is nothing before our bodies lie there
For there she lies moulding and turning to clay.
    —d. 1814
        Tarrytown, New York

The sweet remembrance of the just
Shall flourish when they sleep in Dust.
    —d. 1776

PEACE FOR THE FAITHFUL

Go home my wife, dry up your tears,
I am not dead, but sleeping here,
I am not yours, but Christ's alone—
He loved me best, to Him I've gone.
    —Anon.

With Christ, which is far better.
    —d. 1880
        Brompton Cemetery, London

Why should we tremble to convey
Their bodies to the tomb
Where Jesus our dear saviour lay
And left a long perfume.
    —d. 1813
        Cape Cod, Massachusetts

That life is long, which answers life's great end.
    —d. 1821

🪶 LATE BLOOMERS

Alas sweet Blossom short was the
period that thy enlivening virtues
contributed to the Happiness of
those connections,
But O how long have they to mourn the loss of
so much worth and Excellence.
>   —*d. 1830*
>   *Plymouth, Massachusetts*

The bud was spread
To show the rose
Our Saviour smiled
The bud was closed.
>   —*Anon.*

He plucked me like a tender flower
From this world of faded light,
To dwell among the angels,
Up in heaven so fair and bright.
>   —*d. 1859*

ELOQUENT TRIBUTES

Richly embalm'd indeed thou art,
In the Mausoleum of the heart.
    —*d. 1851, Nantucket, Massachusetts*

Beneath this stone the best of parents lies,
In friendship constant, and in knowledge wise;
They died in humble hope, their trust in God—
O may we follow in the steps they trod.
    —*d. 1864*
      Hillingdon, Middlesex

I came in the morning—it was Spring,
  And I smiled,
I walked out at noon—it was Summer,
  And I was glad,
I sat me down at even—it was Autumn,
  And I was sad,
I laid me down at night—it was Winter,
  And I slept.
    —*Massachusetts*

The dame that rests within this tomb
Had Rachel's beauty, Leah's fruitful womb,
Abigail's wisdom, Lydia's faithful heart,
Martha's just care and Mary's better part.
—*d. 1750*

Who with all his faults
Loved his family and his fellow man.
—*Belstead, Suffolk*

He that's here interred needs no versifying;
A virtuous life will keep the name from dying;
He'll live though poets cease their scribbling rhyme,
When that this stone shall moulder'd be by time.
—*d. 1709*

Behold we see while here we look
The nearest ties of friendship broke
The grief and sorrow pain the heart
The dearest friends we see most part.
—*d. 1849*

II

TOMBSTONE WIT

*Humorous and
irreverent epitaphs*

MINIMALIST TRIBUTES

Here's the last end of the Mortal Story
He's Dead.
—*Daniel Hoar, d. 1773, aged 93*

The Chisel Can't Help Her Any.
—*Anon.*

Molly tho' pleasant in her day
Was suddenly seized and went away
How soon she's ripe, how soon she's rotten
Laid in her grave and soon forgotten.
—*d. 1792*

The Lord don't make any mistakes.
—*d. 1904*

Now Ain't That Too Bad.
—*d. 1907*

She lived—what more can then be said:
She died—and all we know she's dead.
　　—d. 1836

Came in,
Walked about,
Didn't like it,
Walked out.
　　—Suffolk

Died of thin shoes.
　　—d. 1839

He sowed, others reaped.
　　—d. 1895

My dear and beloved Wife
Thou has left me to mourn thy sad loss
　And by the Blessing of God and Son,
I found another Wife.
　　—Anon.

Going, But Know Not Where.
  —*d. 1918*

Gone home.
  —*Anon.*

Charles Lewis.
He voted for Abraham Lincoln.
  —*Anon.*

Been Here
and Gone There.
Had a Good Time.
  —*d. 1916*

She never done a thing to
displease her Husband.
  —*d. 1859*

UNHAPPY ACCIDENTS

Here lies the body of Susan Lowder
Who burst while drinking a Sedlitz Powder.
Called from this world to her heavenly rest,
She should have waited till it effervesced.

> —*d. 1798*
> *Massachusetts*

Always tidy, neat and clean.
Lost his life in a submarine.

> —*Anon.*

Here lie I and my three daughters,
All from drinking the Cheltenham waters.
While if we had kept to the Epsom salts,
We should not now be in these here vaults.

> —*Anon.*

Here lies the body of Emily White,
She signaled left, and then turned right.

> —*Anon.*

Wherever you be
Let your wind go free.
For it was keeping it in
That was the death of me.
  —*Anon.*

Eliza, sorrowing, rears this marble slab
To her dear John, who died of eating crab.
  —*Pennsylvania*

Alas Poor Willie is dead,
His friends know him no more,
For what he thought was H_2O
Proved H_2SO_4.
  —*d. 1982*

The boiling coffee did on me fall,
And by it I was slain,
But Christ has brought my liberty,
And in Him I'll rise again.
  —*Anon.*

The apple wheel did roll on me
And by it I was slain,
But Christ has brought my liberty,
In Him I'll rise again.
    —d. 1799

To all my friends I bid adieu;
A more sudden death you never knew:
As I was leading the old mare to drink,
She kicked and killed him quicker'n a wink.
    —Anon.

Daniel Chappell
Who was killed in the act
of taking a whale.
    —d. 1845

Here lies cut down like unripe fruit;
The wife of deacon Amos Shute;
She died of drinking too much coffee,
Anny Dominy Eighteen forty.
    —d. 1840

She was not smart, she was not fair,
But tears with grief for her are swellin';
And empty stands her little chair—
She died of eatin' watermelin.
        —*Anon.*

Here lies one whose life threads cut asunder
She was stroke dead by a clap of thunder.
        —*d. 1719*

Here I lie and no wonder I'm dead,
I fell from a tree,
Roll'd over dead.
        —*d. 1824*

In Memory of Samuel Barns,
Son of Mr. Samuel Barns
and Mrs. Welthy Barns,
whose Death was Occasion'd
by a Scald from a Tea pot.
        —*d. 1794*
          New Haven, Connecticut

🪽 HELPED TO THE GRAVE

Here lies the body of Jonathan Tilton
Whose friends reduced him to a skeleton.
They robbed him out of all he had
And now rejoice that he is dead.
    —*d. 1837*

Mr. Gilman Spaulding
Was kill'd with an axe
By an insane Brother.
    —*d. 1842*

Think my friends when this you see
How my wife has done for me
She in some oysters did prepare
Some poison for my lot and fare
Then of the same I did partake
And Nature yielded to its fate.
Before she my wife became
Mary Felton was her name.
    —*d. 1860 (from arsenic poisoning)*

THE LAST WORD

Bury me not when I am dead
Lay me not down in a dusty bed
I could not bear the life down there
With earth worms creeping through my hair.
—*d. 1883*

I told you I was sick.
—*Anon.*

My life's been hard
And all things show it;
I always thought so
And now I know it.
—*d. 1915*

Here lie I by the churchyard door.
Here lie I because I'm poor.
The farther in, the more you pay,
But here lie I as warm as they.
—*Anon.*

🪽 PUNS AND RHYMES

In Memory of Elizabeth
   who should have been
   the Wife of Mr. Simeon Palmer.
In Memory of Lidia
   ye Wife of Mr. Simeon Palmer.
     —Twin stones, Rhode Island

Here lies Mary the wife of John Ford,
We hope her soul is gone to the Lord;
But if for Hell she has chang'd this life,
She had better be there than be John Ford's wife.
     —d. 1790

He bowled his best but was himself bowled by the
best on July 2nd, 1912.
     —Tom Richardson, England cricketer, d. 1912

Here lies Will Smith—and, what's something rarish,
He was born, bred, and hanged, all in the same parish.
     —Anon.

Here beneath this stone there lies,
Waiting a summons to the skies,
The body of Samuel Jinking.

He was an honest Christian man,
His fault was that he took and ran
Suddenly to drinking.
Whoever reads this tablet o'er,
Take warning now and drink no more.
  —Maine

A zealous Locksmith died of late,
And did arrive at heaven's gate;
He stood without and would not knock,
Because he meant to pick the lock.
  —Anon.

By spots he died tho' spotless was his life.
  —d. 1767

He is filling his last cavity.
  —Dentist

Here lies John Auricular,
Who in the ways of the Lord walked perpendicular.
— *New England*

Under the sod and under the trees
Lies the body of Jonathan Pease.
He is not here, there's only the pod:
Pease shelled out and went to God.
— *d. 1880*
Nantucket, Massachusetts

Here lies John Yeast.
Pardon me for not rising.
— *Anon.*

My Trip is Ended.
Send My Samples Home.
— *Salesman, d. 1862*

This is on me.
— *d. 1939*

HASTY CHISELS

Gone to be an angle.
— *Should read "angel"*

My virtue liv's beyond the grave
My glass is rum.
— *Should read "run"*

Lord she is thin.
— *Should read "thine"*

· III ·

CARVED
IN STONE

Unique mementoes

🪽 SINS AND OMISSIONS

He meant well,
Tried a little, Failed much.
     —*d. 1889*

She was good but not brilliant,
Useful but not great.
     —*d. 1807*

Those that knew him best deplored him most.
     —*d. 1836*

Here lies as silent clay
Miss Arabella Young
Who on the 21st of May
Began to hold her tongue.
     —*Hatfield, Massachusetts*

She sleeps alone at last.
     —*Anon.*

He was literally a father to all the children of the parish.
—*Anon.*

At rest beneath the churchyard stone
Lies stingy Jeremy Wyatt.
He died one morning just at ten
And saved a dinner by it.
—*Studley, Wiltshire*

Here lies "old thirty-five percent"
The more he made, the more he lent;
The more he got, the more he craved;
The more he made, the more he shaved;
Great God! can such a soul be saved.
—*Money lender, San Francisco*

Her temper was furious
Her tongue was vindictive,
She resented a look and frowned at a smile,
And was as sour as vinegar.
She punished the earth upwards of 40 years,
To say nothing of her relations.
—*Massachusetts*

🜨 READER, REPENT

Man comes into the world naked and bare
He travels through life with trouble and care
His exit from the world no one knows where
If it's well with him here, it is well with him there.
—*d. 1817*

There was hope in his end.
May there be hope in thine.
—*d. 1803*

Weep not for me, for it is in vain,
Weep for your sins, and then refrain.
—*d. 1708*

Keep death and judgement always in your eye,
Or else the devil off with you will fly,
And in his kiln with brimstone ever fry:
If you neglect the narrow road to seek,
Christ will reject you, like a half-burnt brick!
—*Anon.*

🪽 CARPE DIEM

Seize the moments while they stay,
Seize them, use them,
Lest you lose them,
And lament the wasted day.
    —*Anon.*

Seize, mortals, seize the transient hour;
Improve each moment as it flies;
Life's a short Summer, man a flower;
He dies, Alas! how soon he dies.
    —*d. 1816*

Go Reader,
And in the short Space of Life allotted thee
Attend to his Examples
And Imitate his Virtues.
    —*d. 1775, New Haven, Connecticut*

Be thou what you think I ought to have been.
    —*Anon.*

MIND YOUR OWN BUSINESS

Reader pass on and ne'er waste your time,
On bad biography and bitter rhyme
For what I am this cumb'rous clay insures,
And what I was, is no affair of yours.
        —*d. 1797*

Those who cared for him while living
will know whose body is buried here.
To others it does not matter.
        —*Hartford, Connecticut*

I was somebody.
Who, is no business
of yours.
        —*Stowe, Vermont*

🪶 TOMB IT MAY CONCERN

Behold and See
For as I am So shalt Thou Be
But as Thou Art
So Once Was I
Be Sure of This
That Thou Must Die.
      —*d. 1709*

One Night awaits us all;
Death's road we all must go.
      —*d. 1752 (quotation from Horace)*

Here lies interred a blooming youth,
Who lived in love and died in truth.
Behold and see as you pass by,
As you are now so once was I,
As I am now so you must be;
Prepare for death and follow me.
      —*d. 1794*

A sov'reign God, who set my bounds,
Did quickly take my breath.
Be ready then each hour you live
To meet an instant death.
    —*d. 1791*

M y time is come—Next may be thine
Prepare for it whilst thou has time
And that thou mayst prepared be
Live unto Him who died for thee.
    —*d. 1874*

R emember this as you walk round,
All must return into the ground;
For by transgression in the garden
Adam did receive his warning;
And as God's word does prove true,
I have returned, and so must you.
    —*Ridgefield, Connecticut*

O reader be prepared.
    —*Anon.*

DISBELIEVERS

Where is God?
— *d. 1895*

Beyond the universe there is nothing and within the
universe the supernatural does not and cannot exist.
Of all deceivers who have plagued mankind, none are
so deeply ruinous to human happiness as those
imposters who pretend to lead by a light above nature.
— *George F. Spencer, d. 1808*
  Lyndon Center, Vermont

Science has never killed or persecuted a single
person for doubting or denying its teaching,
and most of these teachings have been true;
but religion has murdered millions for doubting
or denying her dogmas and most of these dogmas
have been false.
— *Gratis P. Spencer, d. 1908*
  Lyndon Center, Vermont

VICTIMS

George Johnson
Hanged by Mistake.
  —*Anon.*

Accused of witchcraft
She declared
'I am innocent and God will
clear my innocency.'
  —*Rebecca Nurse, d. 1692*
    Accused of witchcraft, hanged in Salem, Massachusetts

God wills us free—Man wills us slaves
I will as God wills: God's will be done.
  Here lies the body of
    John Jack
  A native of Africa who died
March 1773, aged about sixty years.
  —*Concord, Massachusetts*

Persecuted for wearing the beard.
  —*Joseph Palmer, d. 1873*

LIFE'S WORK

Having had 13 children
101 grand-children
274 great-grand-children
49 great-great-grand-children
410 Total. 336 survived her.
    —*d. 1768*

Five times five years I lived a virgin's life
Nine times five years I lived a virtuous wife;
Wearied of this mortal life, I rest.
    —*d. 1888*

My sledge and hammer be reclined
My bellows too have lost their wind;
My fire's extinguished, forge decay'd
And in the dust my vice is laid.
My iron's spent, my coals are gone,
The last nail's drove, my work is done.
    —*Ironmonger, d. 1826*

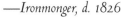

🪽 FIRST PERSON

My life's been short
My soul has fled
And I am numbered
With the dead.
  —*Anon.*

I dreamt that buried in my fellow clay
Close by a common beggar's side I lay;
Such a mean companion hurt my pride
And like a corpse of consequence I cried:
Scoundrel, begone, and henceforth touch me not,
More manners learn, and at a distance rot.
Scoundrel, in still haughtier tones cried he,
Proud lump of earth, I scorn thy words and thee:
All here are equal, thy place now is mine;
This is my rotting place, and that is thine.
  —*d. 1835*
    Providence, Rhode Island

Anything for a change.
  —*Anon.*

· IV ·

FAMOUS
LAST WORDS

*Final tributes to
the famous and infamous*

🕊 MOVERS AND SHAKERS

The Philosophers have only
Interpreted the World in
Various Ways. The point
However is to change it.
       —Karl Marx, d. 1883
           Highgate Cemetery, London
           from Theses on Feuerbach

FREE AT LAST, FREE AT LAST
THANK GOD ALMIGHTY
I'M FREE AT LAST.
       —Reverend Dr. Martin Luther King, Jr., d. 1968
           South View Cemetery, Atlanta, Georgia.

Patriotism is not enough
I must have no hatred or
Bitterness for anyone.
       —Dame Edith Cavell, d. 1915
           British Red Cross nurse in World War II

Reader—Should you reflect on his errors
Remember his many virtues
And that he was a mortal.
—*Sir Walter Raleigh, d. 1618*

Here lies an honest lawyer,—
That is Strange.
—*Sir John Strange, d. 1754*
Master of the Rolls

For beauty, wit, for sterling sense,
For temper mild, for eloquence,
For courage bold, for things wartegan,
He was the glory of Moheagan—
Whose death has caused great lamentation
Both to ye English and ye Indian Nation.
—*Samuel Uncas, Mohegan chief.*

Tell my children to obey the laws and uphold the
Constitution.
—*Judge Stephen A. Douglass, d. 1866*
Chicago, Illinois

To the memory of the Man, first in war, first in peace, and first in the hearts of his countrymen.
—*George Washington, d. 1779*
Mount Vernon, Virginia

David Rice Atchison
1807–1886
President of the U.S. one day
—*Missouri (served as acting president for one day, March 4, 1849)*

"With Malice Towards None."
LINCOLN
"With Charity To All"
—*Abraham Lincoln, d. 1865*
from his second inaugural address

Safe lodged within his blanket, here below,
Lie the last relics of old Orono;
Worn down with toil and care, he in a trice
Exchanged his wigwam for a paradise.
—*Orono, d. 1801, Penobscot chief*

🕊 LITERARY LINES

Here lies one whose name was writ in water.
　　—*John Keats, d. 1821*

Beneath this stone a Poet Laureate lies,
Nor great, nor good, nor foolish, nor yet wise;
Not meanly humble, nor yet swell'd with pride,
He simply liv'd—and just as simply died:
Each year his Muse produc'd a Birth-Day Ode,
Compos'd with flattery in the usual mode:
For this, and but for this, to George's praise,
The Bard was pension'd and received the bays.
　　—*William Whitehead*

"Nothing of him that doth fade
But doth suffer a sea-change
Into something rich and strange."
　　—*Percy Bysshe Shelley, d. 1822*
　　　from Shakespeare's The Tempest

Excuse my dust.
> —*Dorothy Parker, d. 1967*

Time held me green and dying
Though I sang in my chains like the sea...
> —*Dylan Thomas, d. 1953*
>> *Poet's Corner, Westminster Abbey, London, from "Fern Hill"*

Underneath this stone doth lie
As much beauty as could die.
> —*from Ben Jonson's "Epitaph for Lady H"*

Under the wide and starry sky
Dig the grave and let me die.
Glad did I live and gladly die,
And I laid me down with a will.
   This be the verse you grave for me:
Here he lies where he longed to be;
Home is the sailor, home from the sea
And the hunter home from the hill.
> —*Robert Louis Stevenson, d. 1894*
>> *from "Requiem"*

Their grief is in proportion to their affection,
they know their loss to be irreparable,
but in their deepest affliction they are consoled
by a firm though humble hope that her charity,
devotion, faith and purity, rendered
her soul acceptable in the sight of her
REDEEMER.

—*Jane Austen, d. 1817*

Good friend for Jesus sake forbeare,
To dig the dust encloased heare:
Bleste be ye man [tha]t spare these stones,
And curst be he [tha]t moves my bones.

—*William Shakespeare, d. 1616*
Stratford-upon-Avon

Warm summer sun, shine kindly here;
Warm southern wind, blow softly here;
Green sod above, lie light, lie light—
Good-night, dear heart, good-night, good-night.

—*Olivia Susan Clemens, d. 1890*
Written by her father, Mark Twain

THE LAST WORD

"Quoth the Raven nevermore."
—*Edgar Allen Poe, d. 1875*
  from "The Raven"

If I should die, think only this of me:
That there's some corner of a foreign field
That is forever England. There shall be
In that rich earth a richer dust concealed;
A dust whom England bore, shaped, made aware,
Gave, once, her flowers to love, her ways to Roam,

A body of England's, breathing English air,
Washed by the rivers, blest by suns of home.
And think, this heart, all evil shed away,
A pulse in the eternal mind, no less
Gives Somewhere back the thoughts by England
Given;
Her sights and sounds; dreams happy as her day;
And laughter, learnt of friends; and Gentleness
In hearts at peace, under an English heaven.
        —*Rupert Brooke, d. 1915*
          from "The Soldier"

THAT'S ENTERTAINMENT

I never met a man I didn't like.
—*Will Rogers, d. 1935*

Here lies Groucho Marx
and Lies and Lies and Lies.
PS. He never kissed an ugly girl.
—*Groucho Marx, d. 1977*
from The Secret Word is Groucho

If I take the Wings of the Morning,
and Dwell in the Uttermost Parts of the Sea.
—Charles Lindbergh, d. 1974
from The Old Testament, Book of Psalms 139:9

May The Divine Spirit That Animated
Babe Ruth To Win the Crucial Game of Life
Inspire the Youth of America!
—*George Herman ("Babe") Ruth, d. 1948*

🪶 LOST LEGENDS

First to go
through the Whirlpool
Rapids in a
barrel and live.
    —*Carlisle D. Graham, d. 1886,*
        Niagara Falls, New York

Prof. Holden
the old Astronomer
discovered that the Earth
is flat and stationary
and that the sun and moon
do move.
    —*Joseph W. Holden, d. 1900*

In memeori ov
Meri Pitman
Weif ov Mr. Eizak Pitman
Fonetik Printer, ov this Siti.
        —*d. 1897*
            Wife of Isaac Pitman, inventor of shorthand